EDITOR'S NOTES

The script for The Firesign Theatre's "Nick Danger"
is presented in the manner of a 1940s-50s radio script,
with lines of dialogue and indications for live sound
effects and music cues.

Firesign has often staged the piece in the manner
of a Golden Age broadcast, alternating in the roles
of Nancy and the Sound Effects Man, using funny
costumes, scripts and microphones.

Other productions of "Nick Danger" have broken free
of the radio format and radio conventions (as does the
script itself) and turned the piece into a surreal stage
comedy.

Productions need both a keyboardist and a SFX artist.
Beyond that, cast can go from four to six or more.

A lot of the humor comes from the "off-mike"
interactions among the cast members and particularly
from the ornery nature of the actor playing
Catherwood, who continually ad libs to disrupt the
continuity of the show. Timing is all.

The sound effects themselves should be comic in
nature and the person who performs the effects can
also be a merry prankster or a befuddled walk-in.
Objects mentioned, like cellophane and cornstarch, are
references to early live sound effects.

The original Hammond B3 studio organ sound can be duplicated by contemporary keyboards. The original *Nick Danger* theme was based on a jolly tune from a W C Fields movie, *Million Dollar Legs*. The mood can be moody too, in the *Harlem Nocturne* manner.

THE FIRESIGN THEATRE:

THE FURTHER ADVENTURES OF NICK DANGER, THIRD EYE

Phil Austin, Peter Bergman,
David Ossman & Phil Proctor
stage edition edited by
David Ossman

BROADWAY PLAY PUBLISHING INC
New York
www.broadwayplaypublishing.com
info@broadwayplaypublishing.com

Cover art by William Stout
First printing: February 2012
I S B N: 978-0-88145-509-0
Book design: Marie Donovan
Page make-up: Adobe InDesign
Typeface: Palatino
Printed and bound in the U S A

A NOTE ON SOUND EFFECTS

The sound effects and their performance are basic to the comedy of NICK DANGER. Here's how we did it: all the effects were arranged on a table to the side of the performers on microphone. The effects were, of course, also miked, and often done very close "on mike" for maximum effect.

Sound-effects tell a story and have a beginning, a middle and an end. The listener's ear will follow the story if the effect is presented clearly and has a chance to evolve into a familiar sound from the real world.

The script mentions cornstarch (for the sound of walking in snow) and cellophane (for a crackling fire). e've substituted plastic bubble-wrap and other silly things for the fire, but for the snow effect, there's nothing like an unopened box of super-market cornstarch, pressed with the thumbs close on mike. Here are some other choices for the performers and the SFX table:

FOGHORN— Live vocal effect— "Beeee-ohhhh!"

FOOTSTEPS— A pair of hard-soled man's shoes (and a high-heeled pair for Nancy) can be "walked" on various surfaces—wood, concrete slab, kitty litter box filed with sand, gravel or litter. A little practice will make the walking both funny and convincing, even running up or down stairs.

TELEPHONE— It's an old fashioned phone and phone bell. The best thing is to acquire a real heavy 1940s-style telephone and build a ringer (it can be a doorbell too) that plugs in and is operated by hand.

"PHONE EFFECT"— The person on the far end of the telephone needs to sound "pinched." This can be done by speaking into a largish paper cup, the cup just open to the microphone.

NICK'S "NARRATION" VOICE— These are Nick's inner thoughts. Phil Austin simply spoke through his cupped hands.

THUNDER— Make a Thunder Balloon by putting about a half-cup of copper shot inside a large, thick-skinned balloon. Blown up, the balloon should be at least 18 inches in diameter. Roll the shot around inside the balloon several times, then quickly "shoot" the balloon firmly at, and ending close to the mike. This will create a loud, thunder-like explosion, which then tails off as you roll the shot around and fade away from the microphone. Wherever the script calls for rain out of doors, use the Thunder Balloon and lots of drops on a softer surface. (Here's a tricky effect for the Balloon. If you include a couple of spoonfuls of a white powdery substance inside the balloon and, with a tack, pop the balloon at the appropriate moment, the burst of powder will provide a moment of shock and awe.

RAIN ON THE DESK— Could be almost anything "dripped" onto a wooden surface. Experiment for the best effect.

DOORS— A four-foot high (or full-size) prop door with squeaky hinges, a knob that can be rattled and which closes with a satisfying "thunk" is the beautiful solution. Lacking that, an actor can imitate the "cur-click" of a door latch and the "ker-slam" of a door's closing.

PAPER BAG— A real bag, of course. With a pickle in it.

NANCY'S RING— Any cheap and silly sound made by dropping an object onto a wood surface.

CRICKETS AND NIGHTSOUNDS— A cliché of Old Time Radio was "crickets and owls for nighttime, singing birds for daytime." These can be vocally simulated, with or without props.

PAPER RUSTLING— Most paper rustling sounds can be simply done by rustling the pages of a script.

PEN SCRATCHING— Do this close up on mike.

DIAL TONE— A vocal effect, done by Nancy.

TRAFFIC— Vocal horn honks and car drive-bys.

CAR STARTING AND DRIVING— We've usually done all of these vocally.

HITS AND FALLS— Coordinate punches to hand or other surface with the actor's vocal reactions. The SFX person actually falling to the floor might be funnier than dropping a medium-sized sandbag. Or both.

CRASHES— It's convenient to have an all-purpose Crash Box. A safely-taped up sturdy paper box, half-filled with broken glass, crockery, some metal objects and whatever, can be dropped, rolled over, shaken and kicked around until it's no longer safe. Then make another one. Nothing on the SFX table should actually be broken. Keep loud crashes away from the microphone.

HIT ON HEAD— Use a head of lettuce, cabbage or a melon as the skull and fill the toe of a heavy sock with left-over copper shot from the Thunder Balloon. Whack the "head"!

FIGHT SCENES— The hitting effects are coordinated with grunts and groans from the actors. Something might fall over during the fight (a small table with metal objects, perhaps). Each fight should have its own comic reality.

GUNSHOT— Very effective is to find the right combination of a flat stick and a leather or plastic surface (a cushion, for example). Hit the cushion with the stick until you've got a effective and solid "crack!" And, I know, real guns don't sound like that.

LAB SOUNDS— Bubbling retorts are easily simulated by blowing a straw into a cup of thickish liquid. Other "beeps" and such can be found on various digital gadgets and added. The Time Machine can be anything that tells the story: vlock ticks (use a metronome), electrical beeps and waves, a comedy "wanger," you name it.

(Sound: foghorn and footsteps under)

ANNOUNCER: Los Angeles... He walks again by night...

(NICK whistling under)

ANNOUNCER: Out of the fog...into the smog... relentlessly, ruthlessly...

NICK: *(Coughing)* I wonder where Ruth is?

ANNOUNCER: Doggedly...toward his weekly meeting with the Unknown. At 4th and Drucker he turns left. At Drucker and 4th he turns right. He crosses MacArthur Park and walks into a great sandstone building.

(Sound: NICK walks into side of building.)

NICK: Oh! My nose!

ANNOUNCER: Groping for the door, he steps inside, climbs the thirteen steps to his office...

(Sound: Telephone ringing, off. NICK runs up stairs, opens door. phone rings again.)

ANNOUNCER: He walks in! He's ready for mystery... he's ready for excitement... He's ready for anything! He's...

(Sound: Phone picked up. Woops! Extra ring!)

NICK: Nick Danger, Third Eye!

GEORGE: *(On the phone, from another dimension)* Eh, I want to order a pizza to go, and no anchovies.

NICK: No anchovies? You've got the wrong man. I spell my name Danger!

(Sound: Phone hang up)

GEORGE: *(Still somehow on the phone)* What?

(Music: Nick Danger Theme *in and under)*

ANNOUNCER: The makers of Fantastic Cigarettes, "long in the leaf, short in the can," bring you another true story from the tattered casebook of Nick Danger, Third eye. Let's join him now, in the adventure we call, "Cut 'Em Off At The Past!"

(Music: Theme *up and out)*

NICK: *(Narrating, possibly to his secretary)* Let's get down to business. Uncross those beautiful stems of your, baby. Here's the case I call Number 666. It all began innocently enough, on Tuesday.

(Sound: Thunder [use a thunder baloon] and rain)

NICK: I was sitting in my office that drizzly afternoon, listening to the monotonous staccato of rain on my desktop and reading my name on the glass of my office door—REGNAD KCIN. My secretary lay snoring on the floor, her long, beautiful gams pinioned under the couch...

(Sound: Door opens, footsteps approach.)

NICK: I didn't hear him enter, but my nostrils flared at the smell of his perfume—Pyramid Patchouli. There was only one joker in Los Angeles sensitive enough to wear that scent—and I had to find out who he was!

ROCKY: Good afternoon, Mister Danger. I'm Rocky Rococo.

NICK: Thanks, half-pint. You just saved me a lot of investigative work.

ROCKY: Maybe yes, maybe no. Do you know what this is?

(Sound: Paper bag rustling)

NICK: *(Narrating)* I had to think for a minute. What cruel game was he playing? *(To* ROCKY*)* Uh...that's a brown paper bag.

ROCKY: That's correct. Now, look inside, Mr. Danger. What do you see?

(Sound: More bag)

NICK: That's easy. That's a pickle.

ROCKY: Very good. Now, I think you're ready for this!

(Sound: Ring dropped on NICK*'s desk)*

NICK: Why, that's nothing but a two-bit ring from a Cracker Jack box.

ROCKY: I'll sell it to you for five thousand dollars.

NICK: What kind of a chump do you take me for?

ROCKY: First class!

NICK: That tarnished piece of tin is worthless!

ROCKY: Worthless? *(He laughs, coughing.)* Not to Melanie Haber!

NICK: Melanie Haber?

ROCKY: You may remember her as Audrey Farber!

NICK: Audrey Farber?

ROCKY: Susan Underhill?

NICK: Susan Underhill?

ROCKY: How about Betty Jo Bialowsky?

(Music: A big organ surprise sting)

NICK: Betty Jo Bialowsky! I hadn't heard that name since college. Everyone knew her as "Nancy." Then it all came rushing back to me like the hot kiss at the end of a wet fist! It was Pig Nite at the Ohm Mani Padme Sigma House...

(Music: A nice fox-trot in the background)

(Sound: Crickets and night sounds)

NICK: *We had escaped from the crowd and stood trembling underneath the dwarf maples...*

NANCY: Oh, Nicky! Why, I don't know what to say! This is the most beautiful ring I've ever seen!

NICK: *(Speaking in his youthfulvoice)* Yeah, Nancy—it's really neat! It cost me five thousand dollars!

NANCY: Oh, Nicky! How can I ever repay you?

NICK: Well, gee whiz, Nancy—how about five hundred down and a thirty-six month contract?

NANCY: What?

NICK: Or—you could marry me!

(Music: Suspenseful chords)

(Sound: Night birds)

NANCY: That's impossible, Nick. I can't marry you. I can't even tell you why. Maybe—someday...

NICK: All right, Nancy. I understand. Just sign here.

(Sound: Paper rustling, pen scratching)

NANCY: Oh, Nick! I'll never forgive you for this!

NICK: And I'll never forget you neither, Nancy...

(Music fades out)

NICK: *(Older again)* And that's why I called you today, Nan...I mean, Mrs Haber. Something reminded me of that time so long ago, under the dwarf maples.

NANCY: *(On the phone)* I don't know what prompted you to get in touch with me, but you called just in the nick of time.

NICK: You haven't lost your delicate sense of humor, have you, Nancy?

NANCY: What? Nick, I can't talk to you now. You have to get out here right away! My husband—he... It's the same old place in Santa Barbara, Nicky! Hurry, Nicky! I need you!

(Music: A sting)

(Sound: NANCY hangs up. Dial tone)

NICK: Nancy! I slipped the ring into my nose and the receiver in my pocket and headed for the door quickly.

(Sound: NICK's footsteps)

NICK: But I'd forgotten the little man with the evil grin.

ROCKY: Just a second, Danger! What about my pickle?

NICK: You're lucky you still have your brown paper bag, small change!

(Sound: ROCKY hits NICK with the bag.)

ROCKY: Danger, you haven't seen the last of me!

NICK: No, but the first of you turns my stomach!

(Sound: ROCKY's footsteps running off)

ROCKY: *(Calling back)* You'll be hearing from me again, Danger!

(Sound: NICK's footsteps)

NICK: I headed down the hall in the opposite direction, towards the fire-escape. I hadn't a moment to lose.

BRADSHAW: *(Coming on)* Hey, Danger! Where's the fire?

NICK: In your eyes, Lieutenant Broadshaw!

BRADSHAW: Don't get wise with me, Peeper! You're lucky we didn't burn you on the Anselmo Pederaszy Case.

NICK: Look, you caught him, didn't you?

BRADSHAW: Yeah! But the punk got away, no thanks to you!

NICK: What brings your flat feet sniffing around here now, Copper?

BRADSHAW: Just a friendly word of advice, Danger.

NICK: Yeah? What?

BRADSHAW: Don't go stickin' your big nose in police business!

NICK: Sure, Lieutenant. Is that all?

BRADSHAW: No! Don't talk with your mouth full.

NICK: Okay, Bradshaw.

BRADSHAW: And don't fidget while I talk to you!

NICK: Sure, Lieutenant.

BRADSHAW: *(Fading off)* And don't track mud across my nice, clean kitchen floor!

(Music: Sting!)

NICK: *(Calling back)* Okay!

(Sound: Rain, traffic)

NICK: When I hit the street, the rain had already turned Los Angeles into a mud river. It was a short swim down Alvarado to my convertible...

(Sound: Car starts and drives off, then under:)

NICK: I had to get to Santa Barbara in a big hurry. As I whipped onto Mulholland Drive, the lights were just twinkling on across the San Fernandino Valley. I could barely make them out through the driving rain.

(Sound: Car racing and tires squeeling)

NICK: *(Battling the storm)* Then, a hard right down Big Tajunga Canyon. My tires squeeled as I hit Sepulveeda. A right. A left. A left, another right, a left to the body, a right and into a gas station...

(Sound: Car screeches to a stop. hard rain.)

NICK: Hey, Pop!

POP: (*Slowly coming on*) Alright, alright, hold yer horses, I'm comin'... A-yup?

NICK: Where am I?

POP: You can't get there from here.

NICK: But I'm looking for the same old place.

POP: You must mean the Old Same Place, sonny. It's right out back. Here's the key...

(*Sound: Jingle of key, dropped*)

(*Music: Transition phrase*)

(*Sound: Walking on snow*)

NICK: Four hours later, I parked my car in the carriage house and walked up the grey gravel driveway, between a row of dwarf maples, toward the pillared entrance of the Same Mansion. It had been snowing in Santa Barbara ever since the top of the page, and I had to shake the cornstarch off my mucklucks as I lifted the heavy, obsidian door-knocker...

(*Music: Fades out*)

NICK: Hey, in there! Open up! Your door knocker fell off!

(*Sound: Creaking door slowly opens.*)

CATHERWOOD: What's all this brouhaha?

NICK: Brouhaha? Ha ha ha!

CATHERWOOD: (*Mocks him*) Ha ha ha ha!

NICK: (*Trying to top him*) Ha ha ha ha ha!!

(*Sound: Door slams shut.*)

NICK: Wait a minute! Don't you want this door-knocker?

CATHERWOOD: (*Off, muffled*) I already have one.

NICK: But this is yours!

CATHERWOOD: *(Off)* You see? I told you. We used to have another one, but he vanished mysteriously.

(Sound: Door creaks open)

CATHERWOOD: Alright. Come in out of the cornstarch and dry your mucklucks by the fire.

(Sound: Door slams shut. Fire effect)

CATHERWOOD: Let me introduce myself. I am Nick Danger.

NICK: No, let me introduce myself. I am Nick Danger.

CATHERWOOD: If you're so smart, why don't you pick up your cues faster?

NICK: Are those my cues?

CATHERWOOD: Yes. And they must be dry by now. Why don't you pull them out of the cellophane before they scorch!

(Sound: Fire effect out)

CATHERWOOD: Alright, sir. May I take your hat and goat? I assume you've come to see my mistress, Mister Danger.

NICK: I don't care about your private life, or the way you read your lines! I've come to see Nan...Mrs Haber.

CATHERWOOD: Mrs Haber?

NICK: Audrey Farber?

CATHERWOOD: Audrey Farber?

NICK: How about Betty Jo Bialowsky?

(Music: Sting!)

CATHERWOOD: Oh! You mean Nancy. She's in the aviary, stunting trees. I shall return with her straightaway. You may wait here in the sitting room. *(Going off)* Or, you can sit here in the waiting room...

NICK: There was something fishy about the Butler. I think he was a Pisces, probably working for scale. I felt a thin shiver run up my spine as I sat down on the cold marble floor.

(Sound: A vocal shiver. Whoops!)

NICK: What was it about this place? The atmosphere was as phony as the Tudor balustrade that leered at me from the top of the staircase. And there she stood! Radiant! All those curves showing through that flimsy burnoose.

NANCY: *(Off)* Nick!

(Sound: Running down stairs)

NICK: It was Nancy, running down the stairs. All the familiar sounds and smells of Pig Nite came rushing back like a good snort of Scotch. Then, it struck me...

(Sound: A dull thud)

NICK: *(Passing out)* Twenty years later and she still knocked me out! Ooohhh...

(Sound: Body fall)

(Music: Transition, then under and out)

(Sound: Slapping)

NANCY: Oh, Nick! Nick! Nick, darling!

NICK: *(Groggy)* Where am I?

NANCY: Oh, Nick! Wake up! Are you all right?

NICK: Oh...yes...

NANCY: Then stop slapping me!

(Sound: Slapping stops.)

NICK: Nancy, what's the bird's-eye lowdown on this caper? Whatever that means...

NANCY: *(Muffled)* Nick—we can't talk here. *(Worse)* We can't talk here...

NICK: *(Muffled)* What do you mean, we can't talk here?

NANCY: *(Unintelligable)* Wecan'talkhere!

NICK: *(Same)* Oh, you're right! We can't talk here. What shall we do?

NANCY: *(Garbled)* Follow me. This way.

(Sound: Muffled feetsteps)

(Music: A hymn-like melody plays under)

NANCY: Ah! This is much better. We're in the chapel now. It's soundproof, so no one can her us.

NICK: What did you say?

NANCY: I said, no one can...

NICK: What?

NANCY: Never mind! Follow me.

NICK: What?

NANCY: Here. Take my hand. This way.

(Sound: Feetsteps)

(Music: Transitions out)

NANCY: Ah! This is much better.

NICK: Yeah. Pretty fancy layout you've got here, Nancy. What's this, your boudoir?

NANCY: Oh, no, Nick. These are the kennels.

NICK: Puttin' on the dog, eh? Let's see, where are all the doggies?

NANCY: They've mysteriously disappeared.

NICK: Oh, yeah?

NANCY: Yes. I just told you. Along with the servants. They were very attached to one another.

NICK: Where?

NANCY: At the wrists and ankles.

NICK: Wait a minute! You said all the servants had disappeared!

NANCY: Did I?

NICK: What about your butler?

NANCY: You mean Catherwood?

CATHERWOOD: Yes, Madam?

NANCY: Oh! Catherwood! You startled me.

CATHERWOOD: I'm sorry, Madam.

NANCY: What are you doing on all fours?

CATHERWOOD: I'm looking for my script. Why don't you go on without me?

NICK: Listen, Nancy—I smell a rat!

CATHERWOOD: *(Off)* So do I. I think he's got my script.

NANCY: Yes, Catherwood. You look for it, alright?

CATHERWOOD: *(Off)* Alright, Madam.

NANCY: Nick! Quickly, through this sacred panel!

(Sound: Sliding panel)

(Dialogue has reverb through this scene.)

NANCY: Over here. This way.

NANCY & NICK: This is the Portrait Gallery... *(They laugh.)* This is the Port...

NANCY: *(Laughing)* There's an echo in here.

NICK: ...Echo in here...

NANCY: This is the Portrait Gallery, Nick. It's the safest room in the mansion. No one can find us here.

NICK: Why, Nancy...

NANCY & NICK: *(They cozy up for a while, then:)* Get your hands off me!

NICK: What's the scoop ?

NANCY: Chocolate, butterscotch, or Rocky Rococo... er, Road!

NICK: That reminded me. How had she gotten herself involved with that slimy weasel, Rococo? And—how do I make my voice do this?

NANCY: Oh, K-nicky-Nick-Nick! It all began twenty years ago with the mysterious disappearance of my husband.

NICK: You mean you were already married when I sold you that ring? No wonder she hadn't been able to meet the payments!

NANCY: What?

NICK: So that was your secret! What a sap I've been!

NANCY: Oh, yes! But that night, the strangest thing happened.

NICK: That usually goes along with just being married.

NANCY: My husband—Johnny—he... Oh, Nick, I want to tell you the horrible truth. The whole truth, all of it. The man behind everything...

CATHERWOOD: Tea, Madam?

(NANCY *and* NICK: *gasps of surprise*)

NICK: Let me handle this, Nancy. Uh—far out, Catherwood. Just roll a couple of bombers and leave them on the side table.

CATHERWOOD: Yes, Madam.

(*Sound: Tremendous crash*)

(NANCY *screams and cries hysterically.*)

CATHERWOOD: Oh, I say! Pardon me, Madam. I seem to have crashed. It's been such a long exposition, you know. I'm so tired.

NICK: *(Sobbing along with* NANCY*)* Catherwood! Catherwood! Can't you see you're upsetting Nancy? Leave us alone!

CATHERWOOD: How much would you like, sir? Five hundred? A thousand?

NICK: Amscray, usterbay!

CATHERWOOD: Of course, sir. Goo-goo-goo-joob, sir.

NICK: Gazundheit!

CATHERWOOD: *(Singing, going off)* "I'm so tired, I haven't slept a wink..."

(Sound: Door closes.)

NICK: Alright, Nancy. Go on with your story. Start with your dreadful secret.

NANCY: Oh, Nick, I can't! I can't! I'm so confused!

NICK: Why don't you just hold your thumb next to your lines? See? Like this, look. This way I don't get confused and I don't lose my place.

NANCY: I feel faint! The whole world is spinning!

NICK: Why, that's lucky for us, Nancy. If it were flat, all the Chinese would fall off.

NANCY: Ooooo... *(She faints.)*

(Sound: Body falls to floor)

NICK: Why, she's no fun. She fell right over!

(Music: Sexy theme in and under)

NICK: I'll just wrap her skirt around her head, like this, to keep her warm. Now, I'll press her body close to mine to keep me warm!

*(*NANCY *moans.)*

NICK: She looked so helpless there, spread-eagled on the floor. I beat the eagle off and gave her a quick mouth-to-mouth resuscitation job. And then, it struck me...

(Sound: Dull thud)

NICK: What a sap she had!

(Sound: Body falls to floor. Door opens.)

CATHERWOOD: Ah! Good girl, Nancy! That ought to hold him for a while.

NANCY: Oh, poor Nicky. He's bleeding. I'll tear this strip off my petticoat...

CATHERWOOD: If you want to...

(Sound: Ripping of cloth)

NANCY: There! You tie him up with this, while I go through his pockets.

CATHERWOOD: Alright...

(NICK groans.)

CATHERWOOD: Careful! Careful! Don't wake him up.

NANCY: That contract must be on him somewhere.

NICK: *(Unconscious)* ...Audrey...

(Sound: Door opens.)

ROCKY: You fools! Haven't you found the contract yet? Your time is almost up!

CATHERWOOD: Rococo! You slimy blackmailer! How did you get in here? You don't have a key.

ROCKY: No, only half a key. I had to split it with the Sound Effects Man.

SFX MAN: *(Off)* Thanks, Rocky!

ROCKY: Where is the contract, you absent-minded old frog?

NANCY: Wait a minute! Wait a minute! Here it is! I've found it! It was taped to his leg.

ROCKY: Give me that! Ha ha! I've got it at last!

(Music: A big sting!)

CATHERWOOD: Alright! Now, maybe you'll leave us in peace, Rococo! Give me the negative!

ROCKY: Of course. Here it is.

CATHERWOOD: At last! Now we're out of your evil clutches!

NANCY: Dan! Dan! Wait a minute!

CATHERWOOD: What?

NANCY: Look at this negative! It's an interesting approach, but it isn't us!

CATHERWOOD: Yes, she's right! What are you trying to pull on me, Rococo?

ROCKY: Oh, my goodness! I must have sent the wrong negative to the police! I mean...I must have left yours in the car. I'll go get it.

CATHERWOOD: Just a second, Rococo. You're not going nowhere until you've explained what you've done with that filthy piece of blackmail!

ROCKY: Are you threatening me? Why, you stupid toad! I ought to beat your brain out!

NANCY: No! Put down that pickle!

CATHERWOOD: You'll never get away with this, Rococo!

ROCKY: Oh, yeah? *(Continues under NICK)* Didn't you ever see me in *Casablanca*? *Key Largo*? *Mister Moto*? *Crime and Punishment*? *The Maltese Falcon*? *Beat The Devil*? *The Beast With Five Fingers*? You fool!

NICK: *(Narrating over ROCKY)* The thick veil of pain lifted enough for me to eyebsll the situation. Rococo, that sleazy weasel, how did he get in here? And what was he doing with that pickle in one hand and my contract in the other? I had no choice. Nancy and the old butler were frozen with terror. I struggled quietly to my feet and flung myself headfirst at Rococo's stomach!

(Sound: Violent struggle and fight, suddenly over)

NANCY: Thank you, Nick! You saved our lives!

NICK: This is no time for ticker-tape parades, baby. Get me out of these ropes and into a good belt of Scotch.

CATHERWOOD: Let me hold that contract for you, Mister Danger.

(Sound: Rustle of paper)

NICK: I'll keep that contract, Catherwood! But you can take this pickle off my hands.

NANCY: No—er, I think you'd better hold on to that, Nick.

NICK: Good thinking, sweetheart! Lt. Bradshaw will need all the evidence he can get.

CATHERWOOD: Yes. And you should stick around too, Danger. You can help him put all the pieces together, you know.

NICK: Right!

NANCY: No, no. A left!

(Sound: Dull thwack)

(Music: Dizzy sounds under)

NICK: I felt like I was being kicked in the head by the whole chorus line at Minsky's. So Nancy was in on this caper! I felt myself going under. The biggest long-shot Louie at Hialeah wouldn't put a fin on my fate now! This time, something told me I was out for lunch. I even began to hear things...

(Voices swim echoing in NICK's head.)

NANCY: I'll never forgive you, Nick...

BRADSHAW: Keep your nose out of police business...

CATHERWOOD: May I take your hat and goat, sir?...

ROCKY: What about my pickle?...

ANNOUNCER: We'll be back to Nick Danger after this message!

(NICK *screams.*)

(*Music: Dramatic sting up fast and out*)

BRADSHAW: Alright! Hold it right where you are! I'm Lieutenant Bradshaw, with a piece of advice for you. Now, here in the studio, it's all knuckles and know-how, but when the red light goes off, I'm just plain Harry Ames, citizen and weekend father. Now, take a tip from a cop who does—radio work can be just as dirty and exciting as hunting down Public Enemy Number One! So when I get home, my old lady knows what I need, and how! A warm, heaping bowlful of Loostner's Castor Oil Flakes, with real Glycerine Vibra-Foam. It doesn't just wash your mouth out—it cleans the whole system, right on down the line. So come on, you little Rookies, tell your Mom to get on it and do it every day! Just remember what the guys down at the Precinct House sing...

(*Music backs up the* COPS.)

COPS: (*Singing*) Oh...
It ain't no use
If you ain't got the boost!
The boost you get from Loostners!
Loooo-ooo-stners!

ANNOUNCER: The All-Weather Breakfast.

(*Music:* Danger Theme *in and under*)

ANNOUNCER: And now we return you to Act Three of "Nick Danger, Third Eye."

(*Music: Up and sting out*)

NICK: When the crazy escalator ride ended, I fought my way back up to the land of the living. I came to, slumped over in the front seat of my own car, lying in a pool of cheap rotgut. I had a head full of ideas that were driving me insane, and a mouthful of cotton candy.

BRADSHAW: You want some more cotton candy, Danger? It might sober you up.

NICK: Oh, my head...Bradshaw, baby! I never thought I'd be happy to see your ugly mug!

BRADSHAW: Save the wisecracks for the warden, Danger! I gotcha this time, and I gotcha good! Get out of that car—if you can stand up—and keep your hands high. I gotcha covered!

NICK: Hey, what's this all about, Bradshaw? You know I never carry a rod.

BRADSHAW: Yeah, but it's murder what some people can do with a car. And I got witnesses to prove it!

NANCY: There's the man! Keep me away from him! He did it!

NICK: I don't know why you're doing this, Nancy, but it doesn't change my feelings about you.

NANCY: Oh, Nick, you're such a tool! He did it! He did it!

BRADSHAW: Aw'right! Take it easy, little lady. Now let's get these facts straight. Take this down, Blootwurst. Okay, Professor, how did it happen?

CATHERWOOD: Well, Sergeant...

BRADSHAW: Lieutenant!

CATHERWOOD: Yes. Mrs. Farber and I were sitting right here in the living room, engaged in a friendly round of spin the pickle, weren't we dear? Yes. With our good friend, Mr. Rococo. Then, suddenly, the door flew open and this drunken madman here drove in, honking wildly and heading straight for us!

NICK: He's lying, Bradshaw!

BRADSHAW: Can it, Danger!

CATHERWOOD: Yes! At the last possible moment, he stopped on a dime!

BRADSHAW: I see...

CATHERWOOD: Unfortunately, the dime was in Mister Rococo's pocket.

NICK: I'm going to break your neck, Catherwood!

BRADSHAW: Aw'right! Hold it, Danger! I've heard enough! We'll get the rest of the story from you down at the station house. I've been waiting for this for years!

NICK: Wise up, Bradshaw! I didn't do it!

BRADSHAW: Week in and week out, playing second fiddle while you get all the girls. I'm tired of being Mr. Nice Guy, see! There's gonna be some changes made! Next week this show is gonna be called...

(Music: martial theme under)

ANNOUNCER: "Sergeant Bradshaw, District Attorney!"

BRADSHAW: "Lieutenant!" And I'm gonna have my own theme music! And it's all gonna take place in Washington D C! No plots, just girls and guys, doing nice, simple things, up against Nazis and Fifth Columnists. *(He continues, fading under NICK's narration)* I'll get my name in the papers. My picture taken with Col. Lindberg and Happy Chandler and J Edgar...

NICK: I saw my chance and I took it. Bradshaw would never listen to my story now. It had more holes in it than Albert Hall. My only way out was—like this!

(Sound: Terrific fight between NICK and BRADSHAW)

NICK: *(Breathing hard)* Alright, everybody! Hold it! Catherwood, stop it! I've got Bradshaw's rod pressed against Nancy's temple. Now, you spill the beans or I'll blow her brain out!

CATHERWOOD: I think you're bluffing, flatfoot.

(Sound: Pistol shot and thud of falling body)

CATHERWOOD: No, you weren't bluffing.

NICK: Alright, talk!

(Music: Etherial, flash-back theme)

CATHERWOOD: It all began twenty years ago. I was a freshman in college then, although you would hardly believe it to look at me now. I had just completed work on my science project, and I invited Nancy down to reveal the secret to her...

(Sound: Bubbling chemicals, elecrical zaps)

CATHERWOOD: *(His young voice)* Well, this is it, Nancy. How do you like it?

NANCY: *(Her young voice)* So this is where you've been every night since we got married.

CATHERWOOD: Sure is!

NANCY: Nicky, I thought you were...

CATHERWOOD: It's Danny. But don't say it, Nancy. I know it's been hard, but I wanted to give you the swellest honeymoon a girl has ever had. We're going to grease...

NANCY: And swim the English Channel?

CATHERWOOD: No, no! To Ancient Greece, "where burning Sappho loved and sang, and stroked the wine-dark sea, in the temple, by the moonlight, wa-da-doo-dah!"

NANCY: What?

CATHERWOOD: Don't you see, Nancy? I've built the perfect Time Machine!

NANCY: Oh! It sounds dangerous!

CATHERWOOD: Yes! That's why I'm going to try it out first. Now, when I get into this grandfather clock, you hit me over the head with this bottle of Champagne, right here, set the dial for a thousand and put in three dimes. I'll be gone for a thousand years!

NANCY: A thousand! Oh, that's longer than anyone's ever been gone before!

CATHERWOOD: But to you it will seem like only a minute. Very well, my love! Now, forward! Into the Past!

(Sound: Bottle crash, then time machine effect up and fades quickly out)

NANCY: Gee, I hope he gets back before all this dry ice melts.

(Music: Sinister chords)

(Sound: Door opens.)

ROCKY: *(A younger* ROCKY*)* Mrs Haber?

NANCY: Who's that?

ROCKY: I'm Rocky Rococo. You may have seen me loitering around the drugstore, drinking chocolate malted falcons and giving away free high schools.

NANCY: Well, what are you doing here? What do you want?

ROCKY: I'm here for a friend, Mrs. Haber. If you sign a contract, you're supposed to keep up the payments.

NANCY: Oh, you must be a friend of Nick's.

ROCKY: Yes.

NANCY: But he couldn't want his money already! He only gave me the ring last night. I'm wearing it, see?

ROCKY: Yes! That's a very pretty hand you have there! *(Laughs)*

(NANCY screams.)

(Sound: A struggle, interrupted by the time machine effect returning.)

CATHERWOOD: *(Ancient now)* Nancy! Nancy! It's a success! I have proof! I've been to Ancient Greece. Look at this grape!

NANCY: Who are you, old man? And what have you done with my husband?

CATHERWOOD: What do you mean, Nancy? I am your husband.

NANCY: Oh, no! *(Screams and sobs)*

CATHERWOOD: Who's that ugly dwarf with his hand in your mouth?

ROCKY: Rocky Rococo, at your cervix!

NICK: Alright! Alright, Catherwood! I've heard just enough.

CATHERWOOD: What? Listen, I'm telling this story, young man. What are you doing in my flashback?

NICK: Flashback? What are you talking about? Flashb... Alright, all of you. Stay right where you are. Put your thumbs on your place in the script while I figure this out.

(Confused mumbling from everyone)

NICK: So that was her horrible secret! Poor Nancy, married to a man a thousand years old. Now I understood why the servants had disappeared. It was Catherwood who killed Rococo, to protect his wife! My Betty Jo!

(Music: Sting!)

NANCY: Who is he talking to? And how does he make his voice do that?

NICK: Alright, Bradshaw, there's your confession! I hope you got it all down. Bradshaw? Oh! That's right! He's not in this flashback. How do I...I'll skip ahead! No, I can't skip ahead. I'll... Alright, everybody into the Time Machine!

NICK: No, no, no, no! You don't understand how radio works! Now, this is my flashback. All I have to do to return us to the present is fade my voice out like this... and cue the organist...

(Music: Transition, breaking down into confusion)

CATHERWOOD: And you see, here we are. *(Now his voice is doubled)* Oh, my goodness!

BRADSHAW: What's happening? Am I seeing double? There're two of everybody except me!

(Hubbub of voices in confusion)

NICK: *(Voice doubled)* Pandemonium was breaking out all around me...

    NICK 1: Wait a minute! Who are you?

    NICK 2: I was here first!

    NICK 1: You imposter!

    BOTH NICKS: Take that!

(Sound: Fist-fighting and then two body falls)

BETTY JO: Why, that's terrible!

NANCY: You keep away from him, you young hussy!

BETTY JO: Who are you calling a hussy, you old bag?

NANCY: How dare you talk to me like that?

BETTY JO: I can talk to me any way I like!

NANCY: Oh! What nerve! I'm not you! You're me! Twenty years ago!

BETTY JO: What? You have a lot of nerve saying that I'm going to look like that in twenty years!

NANCY: Oh, yeah?

BETTY JO & NANCY: There ain't room enough in this dress for both of us!

(Sound: Fabric tearing)

NANCY: Have at you!

BETTY JO: Gazuntheit!

(The ladies fight and scream, while:)

DAN: This is a bit of fun, isn't it, Catherwood?

CATHERWOOD: Certainly is, Dan. Glad to have someone my own age to talk to after all these years.

DAN: Why don't we sing something?

CATHERWOOD: I've forgotten the key.

DAN: That's all right. I've got a lid out in the car.

CATHERWOOD: Hit it!

(Music accompanies:)

CATHERWOOD & DAN: *(Singing)*
Half-caste woman,
Living a life apart,
Where did your story begin?...

ROCKY: Stop it! Stop it! Stop singing, you fools! Can't you see someone has been crushed here, under this car? Oh, my God! It's me! I don't look at all well! I'm dead! I've been killed! This hasn't happened to me since "M!"

NICK: *(Voice doubled)* I did a quick twenty-twenty on the whole scene. I had thought that I was the only person going insane, but now we were all in this together. I knew what I had to do. I didn't like it, but that had never stopped me before. Alright, everybody! Take off your...

ANNOUNCER: Ladies and gentlemen, we interrupt this regularly scheduled broadcast to bring you a message of national importance, from the White House in Washington, DC. Ladies and gentlemen...

VOICE: *(Off)* Hold it! Hold it...clear! Now, now!

ANNOUNCER: Ladies and gentlemen, the President of the United States.

PRESIDENT: My fellow Americans. This morning, at 6:25 a.m. Pacific Standard Time, combined elements of the Imperial Japanese navy and air force ruthlessly attacked out naval base at Pearl Harbor in the Hawaiian Islands. I have conferred this morning with Congress and the Chiefs of Staff in emergency session. We have reached our rendezvous with destiny! It is our unanimous and irrevocable decision that the United States of America unconditionally surrender. And now, my wife and I would like to return with you for the thrilling conclusion of "Private Nick Danger, Third Eye."

NICK: *(In the middle of a line)* ...Guess I've solved another one for you.

BRADSHAW: Danger, I'll never know how you do it. I was sure I had the goods on ya this time.

NICK: Well, Bradshaw. It's like in The Army, you know. "The Great Prince issues commands, founds states, vests families with fiefs. Inferior people should not be employed."

BRADSHAW: Nick, I can't knock success, but you still put me through too many changes!

(Music: Sting and into Danger Theme *under)*

ANNOUNCER: The makers of Loostner's Castor Oil Flakes and Fantastic Cigarettes—Loostners for the "Smile of Beauty," Fantastics for the "Smile of Success"—have brought you the transcribed adventures of "Nick Danger, Third Eye!" Tune in again next week, same Fire-time, same Fire-station, when Nick Danger meets "The Asphalt Arab!"

(*Music:* Theme *up for close*)

END OF PLAY

www.ingramcontent.com/pod-product-compliance
Lightning Source LLC
Chambersburg PA
CBHW070037110426
42741CB00035B/2801